A
Fearless Journey
to
Motherhood

*Fighting Fear with Faith
during Infertility and Pregnancy*

TIFFANY FINLEY

ISBN-10: 0-692-15897-9

ISBN-13: 978-0-692-15897-5

Scripture quotations marked (NLT) are taken from the Holy Bible, New Living Translation, copyright © 1996, 2004, 2007 by Tyndale House Foundation. Used by permission of Tyndale House Publishers, Inc., Carol Stream, Illinois 60188. All rights reserved.

Editor Services: Jodi Brandon Editorial | JodiBrandonEditorial.com

Design & Publishing Services: London Lane Designs | LondonLaneDesigns.com

Dedication

*A*ll glory, honor, and praise goes to You—my Creator, my Daddy, my God—for allowing my journey to motherhood to push me closer to You. This is for Your glory. I thank You for always seeing in me what I can't see in myself most times. I'm honored that You would trust me with such beautiful women to share Your word with, and direct back to Yourself.

Thank you, Derek and Caleb. Derek, thanks for always being there for me and by my side every step of the way, supporting me, praying with me, being my strength during moments of weakness, and reminding me to keep faith in Daddy-God on our fertility, and life journey. I love you babe.

Caleb, you are a constant reminder of God's faithfulness to me. My journey to holding you in my arms was one of pain, sorrow, frustration, and overwhelming, unexplainable joy. Thank you for all of your hugs, kisses and pushing Mommy closer to God.

My future miracle, this current journey to meeting you has been one of unexpected bumps in the road. You're already so desired and loved by me, your amazing father, and loving big brother. We cannot wait to see your sweet face.

Contents

Fear No More

I've written this book with the hope of helping other women fight fear with faith by relying on the word and promises of God during a time when fear is one of the most common emotions felt and expressed during a journey to motherhood. I know this because I, too, after being diagnosed with polycystic ovarian syndrome (PCOS), 14 months of trying to conceive, two ectopic miscarriages, giving birth prematurely, and currently trusting God for baby number two, struggle with fear. I fear that I will not conceive again. I fear that I will give birth prematurely again. I could go on and on about numerous things that I fear.

However, I've chosen to fight that fear with the truth of God's word. Does this mean that I no longer feel fear? No. Does this mean that I know all that there is to know regarding overcoming feelings of fear? No. But, it does mean that I'm intentional about using the word of God to combat any feeling or emotion that tries to attach itself to me, or make me feel contrary to what God has already spoken concerning my life.

This book began its conception in 2015 as I began sharing

scriptures on social media to fight fear during infertility, pregnancy, and trying to conceive. I wanted to encourage others in the trying to conceive community to meditate on and proclaim the word of God over their specific situations, while fighting fear with faith. As I continued to share and post these daily scriptures and prayer starters, Holy Spirit gently told me, "This is a book you're writing," and prompted me to put it into book form. It may have taken me a few years to be obedient and actually do what He instructed me to do, but here it is!

Use this book over the next 10 days to set aside quiet, devotional time daily to spend with God, getting to know what He's promised you as it relates to motherhood and pregnancy, and seek His presence. So, grab your Bible and meditate on the scriptures, and stand on their truth. There's a place for daily reflection and application, so that you are not only reading the scriptures, but are able to reflect and write out the promises in each scripture. Additionally, use the daily prayer starters to assist you in having a dialogue—not a monologue—with God about your fears surrounding infertility and pregnancy, because He wants to talk back to you. Sit quietly before Him and allow Him to speak to your heart. I pray that after reading this book you're free of fear and it helps you silence the spirit of fear that desires to consume and paralyze you. I pray that it empowers you to begin to fight with faith using the word, tearing down every negative thought and emotion that the enemy tries to use to attack your spirit, mind, body, and faith. Ultimately, upon finishing this book, I hope that it strengthens and deepens your trust, confidence, and faith in God. I pray that you'll stand on His word during your journey to motherhood and begin to understand how praying the word of God, and believing what it says is more powerful than anything working against you.

Day 1

No More Illness, Miscarriage, and Infertility

"You must serve only the Lord your God. If you do, I will bless you with food and water, and I will protect you from illness. There will be no miscarriages or infertility in your land, and I will give you long, full lives."
Exodus 23:25–26 (NLT)

God will always be everything that we need Him to be, including a faithful God who heals from all sickness, illness, and disease. There is no condition that is too difficult, or beyond His ability to heal. You may be reading this thinking, *Yeah, I know He's a healer, but I don't know if He can really heal me and make me fertile again.* Let me reassure you that He can and He will if you want Him to. Exodus 23:25–26 reminds us that when we serve the one and only, true and living God, He blesses our food and water, and will protect us from any and all illness, such as infertility. Not only does He promise to protect us, but He goes on to promise that there will be no miscarriage or infertility in our land, and He will give us long, full lives.

This is His promise to you—His servant, His daughter. Now, I have to ask: Are you going to stand on this truth today? Are you going to profess this promise over your life and believe what He's said? Are you going to trust this promise, and let it settle deep down in your soul and spirit? Will you allow it to wash away that fear that eats at your hope, faith, and confidence in God? I sure hope so. Because, while I know the inability to conceive, getting your period again month after month of trying, and miscarriage and loss after finally getting that BFP (big fat positive) are real, fearful, heartbreaking, and devastating things (because that has been me on several occasions), I also know that my Daddy-God's word will never return to Him empty, but will accomplish what He desires and achieve the purpose for which He sent it (Isaiah 55:11 NLT).

As you pray and meditate during your quiet time today, allow God to fill you with faith in His word and faith in His ability to protect you from infertility and miscarriage as He supernaturally heals and restores your fertility. Your natural mind can't perceive it just yet, but it will catch up as you allow your spirit to agree with His promises spoken in Exodus 23:25–26. You're on a journey of fearless faith that will require that you strengthen that faith muscle. It won't be easy, but it will be worth it as you release the reign of fear concerning pregnancy, infertility, and trying to conceive by exchanging it for a strengthened faith in God.

Reflection & Application

1. What are God's promises to you in Exodus 23:25–26? List them.

2. How can you apply the above promises to your life today?

3. How can you practice walking in faith, instead of fear, today?

Prayer Starter

God, I take joy and rejoice in knowing that nothing is impossible for you. Today I choose to walk in a spirit of fearless faith, because I'm your servant and daughter. As a result, you will bless my food and water, and will protect me from all sickness, illness, and disease. I thank you that there will be no infertility, and miscarriage in my body. I will have a long, full life. Father, thank you in advance for a strengthened faith and bringing my reproductive organs back into alignment with your word. In Jesus' name, amen.

Thoughts & Prayers

Thoughts & Prayers

Day 2

Walk in Perfect Peace

"You will keep in perfect peace
all who trust in you,
all whose thoughts are fixed on you!"
Isaiah 26:3 (NLT)

On my journey of believing God to conceive naturally my second time around (my first pregnancy was conceived via frozen embryo transfer), peace can be hard to walk in most days, as your burning desire to become a mother or having a successful pregnancy is coupled with questions of "what ifs": *What if I never become a mother? What if I get pregnant but miscarry again? What if that pregnancy test is negative? What if my baby is stillborn after carrying him/her full-term?* So much worry consumes and hovers over us before, during, and after pregnancy. (Oh, yes, you still worry about your children after you've birthed them.)

Does it feel like I'm glorifying being a worrier? Trust me, I'm not. I'm trying to help you understand that worry has taken up residence in your heart, and you have no peace. *At all.* Worry and peace can't co-exist. You're either manifesting one or the other in your life. As of today, I would like for it to be the latter. The word of God says that He will keep in peace all who trust Him and keep their thoughts fixed on Him. This means that while pregnancy, infertility, and trying to conceive present many challenges and moments of worry, you don't have to take the bait. Instead, you can choose to trust God's sovereignty: power, control, and authority over your life. See, when we get a clear revelation of God's power, control, and authority in *all* that concerns us, we can let go of worry and fear. Why? Because we know that our lives are in His hands, and He's a good Father at all times. This revelation alone will release a perfect peace in your life, a perfect peace that says, "Regardless of the situation and outcome concerning motherhood, God is in *total* control." That's the true meaning of peace—not the absence of hardship or tough situations, but trust in a good, loving, all-knowing Father who won't abandon you or forget you, and who carries you through all of life's highs and lowest of lows.

As you pray and meditate during your quiet time today, totally surrender and lay that fear at the feet of Jesus. Exchange it for a walk in perfect peace by putting your *total* trust in your Daddy-God. Keep your thoughts fixed on Him and not on the "what ifs." Perfect peace is yours today.

Reflection & Application

1. What does God promise to you in Isaiah 26:3? Write the promise.

2. How can you apply this scripture to your life today?

3. How can you practice walking in perfect peace, instead of fear, today?

Prayer Starter

God, you are sovereign. You know my life's beginning, middle, and end. Therefore, I release all fear, and trust you with the hard times in my life. I thank you in advance for keeping me in perfect peace as I trust you, and keeping my thoughts and mind fixed on you during pregnancy, infertility, and trying to conceive. In Jesus' name, amen.

Thoughts & Prayers

Thoughts & Prayers

Day 3

Pray About Everything

"Don't worry about anything; instead, pray about everything. Tell God what you need, and thank him for all he has done. Then you will experience God's peace, which exceeds anything we can understand. His peace will guard your hearts and minds as you live in Christ Jesus."
Philippians 4:6–7 (NLT)

My journey of really praying about everything began in January 2015, and I was at a point where I desperately desired healing in my body from PCOS (polycystic ovarian syndrome), as my menstrual cycles were few and far between, coming every three or four months. I remember it like it was yesterday. I began seeking God and praying for healing, because I knew that He'd healed so many diseases and opened the wombs of several women throughout the Bible. Surely He could do the same for me this time around if I just prayed and believed. So that's what I began doing.

Weeks later my church had a prayer and healing conference. The minister asked if there was anyone in the room having female reproductive issues. I stood up, and he prayed a prayer of faith for hormonal balance and healthy reproductive health. A week later I received my menstrual cycle, and have every month since that time. However, a month or so later, fear and doubt reared their ugly heads, and I began second-guessing and questioning the supernatural healing that was taking place in my body. That's when the Holy Spirit immediately spoke to remind me: *Your faith has made you well. Yes, you're healed. It's your faith that has given you healing.* I knew that I'd heard "your faith has made you well," in scripture before, so I went on a search and read these two scriptures aloud to myself:

And Jesus said to the man, "Stand up and go. **Your faith has healed you.**" (Luke 17:19 NLT)

And he said to her, **"Daughter, your faith has made you well.** Go in peace. Your suffering is over." (Mark 5:34 NLT)

Furthermore, not only do I now have monthly menstrual cycles, but I'm ovulating on my own; my right, once severely scarred fallopian tube is now completely open (confirmed by my most recent hysterosalpingogram [HSG]); and only my left fallopian tube was diagnosed as blocked. Sisters, prayer about everything works!

You may be wondering where I am on my fertility and trying to conceive journey today. I'm still praying, trusting, and believing God for my predestined miracle number two. I'm going to continue to do what Philippians 4:6–7 instructs me to do: pray about everything. Can and will you pray about everything, today? Will you lay it all—pregnancy, motherhood, infertility, adoption, surrogacy, low ovarian reserve, unexplained infertility, endometriosis, and everything else in between—at the feet of Jesus?

As you pray and meditate during your quiet time today, tell God what you need, and begin to thank Him for what He has already done and will do as a result of your faith-filled prayers. It's your faith that God honors—Your faith in Him to handle all that you bring to Him in prayers. You can't remain in a relationship with an individual whom you don't trust. It doesn't work. Trust Him today. Pray about it all today. When you really begin to pray about it all, and really hand it to Him, that's when unexplainable peace will come and overtake your soul. So, as you pray about everything, making your requests, needs, and desires known to God, know that it's your faith that moves God, just as the 10 men with leprosy and the woman who touched the hem of His garment had faith in His healing power. Maybe you don't desire healing, but you desire His guidance to connect you to the right adoption agency to pursue motherhood. Maybe you just desire a healthy pregnancy after learning that you're pregnant. Whatever you desire, it can be made well in Christ. After all, He told them in the two scriptures above, "It's your faith that's made you well."

Reflection & Application

1. What does God instruct you to do and promise to you in Philippians 4:6–7? List them.

2. How can you apply this scripture to your life today?

3. How can you practice developing a prayer life concerning everything, instead of worrying and walking in fear today?

Prayer Starter

God, I'm so grateful that I don't have to worry about anything concerning my life, even pregnancy, infertility, and trying to conceive, but I can pray instead and give you my concerns, fears, doubts, and worries. I can tell you all about it and make my requests known to you, thanking you in advance. In exchange, you give me peace that will overcome me, and guard my heart and mind. So, Father, I lay at your feet every care and worry concerning my pregnancy, fertility, and trying to conceive. I accept your peace. In Jesus' name, amen!

Thoughts & Prayers

Thoughts & Prayers

Day 4

The Happy Mother

"He gives the childless woman a family,
making her a happy mother.
Praise the LORD!"
Psalms 113:9 (NLT)

Feeling like you'll never conceive as a result of infertility, regardless of the specific diagnosis, is heartbreaking. Feeling like everyone else around you is getting pregnant—"being fruitful and multiplying"—leaves you with feelings of jealousy, anger, disappointment, desperation, and grief. You begin to wonder, *Why on earth is it happening for everyone else, but it's not happening for me, God?* You begin to entertain thoughts of never being a mother or never seeing a positive pregnancy test. Oh, but let me reassure you that, contrary to your belief, He's going to give you the gift of motherhood and make you a happy mother.

Although you may not see how in the natural, and it may not

have manifested yet in the natural, supernaturally God has already promised you motherhood. Psalms 113:9 declares this promise. What does this mean for you? It means that you may not at this very moment be physically holding a baby in your womb or your hands, but it is on the way. You have to profess in faith that you're a happy mother in the making. Yes, a happy mother in the making! The Bible speaks of life and death being in the power of our tongues. Use your words to profess what God has already spoken about you. If He's said that He's going to give you a family, making you a *happy mother*, then profess that promise daily until your natural mind connects with your spirit, and they both align and agree with God's word. This is part of His will for your life. Trust His timing and His will.

As you pray and meditate during your quiet time, fear no more on today. Worry no more on today. Today is the day that you begin speaking God's word over your current situation. You continue to step out of fear into faith. Declare and decree right now: *"I am a happy mother!"*

Reflection & Application

1. What does God promise to you in Psalms 119:3? List them.

2. How can you apply this scripture to your life today?

3. How can you align your professions about motherhood with what God has said on today?

Prayer Starter

God, your word says that you give the barren, childless woman a family, making her a happy mother. So, God, I thank you that I'm fruitful and will conceive my predestined one (baby) in due time according to your will. Lord, I thank you in advance for giving me a family and making me a happy mother! In Jesus' name, amen!

Thoughts & Prayers

Thoughts & Prayers

Day 5

The Promise Keeper

"It was by faith that even Sarah was able to have a child, though she was barren and was too old. She believed that God would keep his promise."
Hebrews 11:11 (NLT)

Many of us are familiar with the story of Sarah. Sarah was the wife of Abraham. She was childless and barren for quite some time before God opened her womb, and gave her and Abraham the gift of parenthood. Abraham had been informed by God that he and Sarah would be the father and mother of many nations and that they'd have a son name Isaac. Sarah, focusing on her natural condition, laughed and didn't believe that God could or would open her womb and give her a child at the appointed time. But, despite the momentary disbelief, she and Abraham went on to have faith in God, and He kept His promise. Abraham was 100 years old when his son Isaac was born to him. Sarah was 90. They were very old in age, but age was not a factor for God.

Have you ever had a Sarah moment? Are you presently having a Sarah moment? It's that moment when God has promised life in your womb, but you chuckle with disbelief because five, 10, maybe 15 years have gone by and you still don't hear anyone calling you "Mom." It's that moment when God sends encouragement or a prophetic word to you through a friend or minister, and you don't quite receive it, because you've been waiting to be a mother so long. I've had Sarah moments. However, like Sarah and Abraham, you have to believe that the promise will be kept to you. Regardless of how old you are or how long you've been trying, God is the opener and closer of your womb. He's the creator and giver of life. He has the last and final word concerning motherhood for your life. Genesis 21:1–2 (NLT) says, "Now the Lord was gracious to Sarah as he had said, and the Lord did for Sarah what he had promise. Sarah became pregnant and bore a son to Abraham in his old age, at the very time God had promised him." Let today's two scriptures affirm your faith today. Allow them to remind you that if He worked miracles back then, and kept promises back then, He *can* and *will* do it again!

As you pray and meditate during your quiet time, know that He's the same God right now that He was back then. He's still the promise keeper. Nothing about Him has changed. So, take Him at His word and allow that word—that promise—to be fulfilled at the appointed time that He has planned for you.

Reflection & Application

1. What does Hebrews 11:11 tell you about Sarah? What does Genesis 21:1–2 tell you about God? Make a list.

2. How can you apply the two scriptures to your life today?

3. How can you take steps in believing the promises of God on today, even when they seem they aren't manifesting as quickly as you'd like?

Prayer Starter

God, you are a faithful God. You are not a liar, and your word will never return to you without accomplishing that which it was sent to accomplish. So, thank you for being a promise keeper. Father, I thank you for reminding me in your word that by faith in you and your power I am able to conceive, despite a diagnosis of infertility or how old I may be. So, just like Sarah, I believe you will keep your promise. In Jesus' name, amen!

Thoughts & Prayers

Thoughts & Prayers

Day 6

Joy and Gladness

"But the angel said, 'Don't be afraid, Zechariah! God has heard your prayer. Your wife, Elizabeth, will give you a son, and you are to name him John. You will have great joy and gladness, and many will rejoice at his birth.'"
Luke 1:13–14 (NLT)

Your day of great joy and gladness over the birth of your baby is soon to come. God has written your beautiful story. I know it doesn't seem so beautiful right now. In fact, it appears dark, dreadful, and depressing. But when He's done, you're going to have a great testimony filled with such joy and gladness. Do you believe that? You have to know that God has heard, and still hears, all of your prayers. He hears every prayer and sees every tear when you don't have words to pray. He loves for you to talk to Him about those uncertainties of your pregnancy, fertility, and trying to conceive journey. He's heard your constant prayer for a child and a healthy pregnancy, and He's going to deliver just as he did for Zechariah and Elizabeth.

Zechariah was at the altar of incense when an angel of the Lord appeared to him to confirm that God had heard his prayers. The angel shared with Him that he and Elizabeth would be the parents of a son named John, they would have great joy and gladness, and many would rejoice at the baby's birth. Zechariah was so unsure about the truth of that statement, although coming from the angel Gabriel, that He asked, "How could I be sure of this? I am an old man and my wife is well in years (Luke 1:18 NLT)." Even back then, they struggled with doubt and how conception would happen considering their circumstances, just as we do in the present day.

However, prayer and faith always disabled the fear and doubt, and the end story was always one of triumph, joy, and gladness. Know that the same triumph, joy, and gladness will be yours on the other side of your journey to motherhood. You will look back over your season of struggle, uncertainty, and fear after giving birth and think, *It was all so worth it. This joy is like no other that I've ever experienced before.* Not only will you rejoice, but others who are close to you will also get to share in the glory of God's faithfulness to you. They will marvel at God's goodness, and see the testament of God's power in your womb and in your arms.

As you pray and mediate during your quiet time, try to see behind the present and look into your future, in which you're caring for and nurturing that baby that God has assigned to you.

Reflection & Application

1. After the angel tells Zechariah that God has heard his prayer, what three things does the angel make known to him about his future? Make a list.

2. How can those three things shared with Zechariah apply to your life today?

3. What feelings and emotions do you envision feeling after the birth of your child? Who will be there? What are they doing? Hold on to that vision.

Prayer Starter

*L*ord, just like Zechariah, I will not be afraid, because I know that you will answer my prayer to conceive and have a healthy pregnancy, just as you answered Zechariah and Elizabeth's prayer for a son. I thank you that I will have great joy and gladness, and will be able to rejoice with close family and friends at my baby's birth. In Jesus' name, amen!

Thoughts & Prayers

Thoughts & Prayers

Day 7

Confident Trust

"They do not fear bad news; they confidently trust the Lord to care for them."
Psalms 112:7 (NLT)

Infertility has a way of developing an expectation for the worst of the worst to happen. I remember when I finally got that big fat positive (BFP). My husband and I were so full of awe. We literally stood in our bathroom crying tears of joy for almost 30 minutes. I'd spent a year and a half desperately purposing motherhood, and we'd finally gotten our prayers answered. Rewind back a year and a half from that joyous moment: I had had two miscarriages, six months apart. Our first angel left us in August 2011 and our second in February 2012. I remember leaving the ladies room and heading back to my office to work when I received a call from the reproductive endocrinologist's office that evening regarding my beta from earlier that day. The nurse told me that my blood test was positive, but my human chorionic gonadotropin (HCG) levels were low at 25. They wanted me to come back for another beta to ensure that my numbers were doubling. I remember getting off the phone with the nurse and immediately caressing my belly, as there was life now growing on the inside of me. I instantly felt like a mother, within seconds. Then, the unthinkable happened: My numbers weren't doubling, and my reproductive endocrinologist was convinced that my pregnancy was the result of an ectopic (tubal) pregnancy and miscarriage, as there was no baby seen during my sonogram. I was devastated! My heart sank, and my spirit was broken. Then ectopic miscarriage number two happened. It left me numb and angry.

When we finally conceived via a frozen embryo transfer (FET) four months later, I was so fearful of another miscarriage. I didn't instantly feel motherly after seeing that positive home pregnancy test; instead, I was happy *and* fearful. Furthermore, I couldn't quite enjoy my pregnancy due to the fear and worry that consumed me. Is this you today? Did you just get your long, anticipated big fat positive (BFP) after years of trying to conceive with an infertility diagnosis? Did you suffer miscarriages, and so you fear this current pregnancy will result in another? Maybe you're not pregnant at all, but fear never experiencing the gift of motherhood due to your diagnosis or your percentage chance of being able to conceive. You just fear bad news. If any of the aforementioned are you, I empathize with you.

However, God has not given you a spirit of fear. Fear is not of

Him, and if you're walking in fear that means that you can't fully trust God to care for you. Psalms 112:7 says that you don't have to fear bad news because you confidently trust a God who's able to care for you during the worst situations. When things are going well, He cares for you. When things are going all wrong, He cares for you. Regardless of what lies ahead of you on this journey to motherhood, take comfort in knowing that God is already aware. Not only is He already aware, He's already there. So, He says to confidently trust in Him. Don't fear. Confidently trust.

Reflection & Application

1. Do you find it difficult to trust God to care for you? Why?

2. How can you apply Psalms 112:7 to your life today?

3. What fears and worries do you have concerning your journey to motherhood at this moment? Make a list and pray, asking God to help you relinquish those fears and confidently trust Him to care for you

Prayer Starter

God, you have not given me a spirit of fear, but of power, love, and a sound mind. I ask that you help me to relinquish all fears, anxieties, and worries concerning my journey to motherhood. Thank you for reminding me in your word that I don't have to fear bad news of any kind during my pregnancy or trying to conceive journey because I can confidently trust you to care for me. Not only do you care for me, but you care for my baby during this pregnancy and when I shall become pregnant. In Jesus' name, amen!

Thoughts & Prayers

Thoughts & Prayers

Day 8

Accept Peace

"I am leaving you with a gift—peace of mind and heart. And the peace I give is a gift the world cannot give. So don't be troubled or afraid."
John 14: 27 (NLT)

Peace is not something that comes easy for me in my natural day-to-day. You see, I'm a meticulous planner by nature. That means that I need to be in control and know what's going to happen, how it's going to happen, when it's going to happen, and where it's going to happen. When my plan is altered by life events beyond my control, I become worried, anxious, and restless. Consequently, I'm no longing walking in the gift of peace given so freely to me by the Father. It becomes nonexistent to me, as I've buried it under my pile of worry, stress, anxiety, frustrations, fears, and doubts. Do these emotions describe what you're experiencing right now as you wait for a healthy baby to be in your arms?

Isaiah 26:3 tells us that God will keep us in perfect when we trust Him, and keep our thoughts on him: "You will keep in perfect peace all who trust in you, all whose thoughts are fixed on you!"

When we confidently trust God, and keep our thoughts on Him, then we can accept His free gift of peace. We can allow it to rest, rule, and abide in our lives daily. We no longer allow it to stay buried under negative thoughts and emotions. We discover a new way to enjoy life, even during the tough, "everything's not going according to plan and I feel like I have no control right now" seasons of waiting and believing for a healthy baby.

Trusting God and intentionally keeping our thoughts fixed on Him will not come easy when you're dealing with the unexpected, but if you make it a priority to grow in your trust of Him and keep your thoughts on Him, it will get easier to accept and choose His peace, rather than worry.

Reflection & Application

1. List the areas of your life in which you need peace the most.

2. What can you do to accept and pursue peace in those areas listed?

3. Meditate on John 14:27 and Isaiah 26:3.

Prayer Starter

God, thank you for the gift of peace. I thank you that because you've given me peace of mind and heart during this time of trusting you to conceive and pregnancy, I don't have to be troubled, worried, fearful, or afraid. I can rest in knowing that your peace sustains me, even during this seemingly difficult time. So, Lord, I receive your peace that was freely given to me by confidently trusting you and keeping my thoughts on you. I will not be afraid. In Jesus' name, amen!

Thoughts & Prayers

Thoughts & Prayers

Day 9

You're in His Hands

"Don't be afraid, for I am with you. Don't be discouraged, for I am your God. I will strengthen you and help you. I will hold you up with my victorious right hand."
Isaiah 41:10 (NLT)

Today, I want you to know that you're in good hands! Your Father is with you reminding you to not be afraid or fearful. He's right there with you, giving you strength during the most mentally, physically, and emotionally exhausting time of your life. He's strengthening you today. He's helping you pick yourself back up and continue. And while He's doing all of that in your life, He's holding you in the middle of His hand.

Read this poem by James Dillet Freeman:

The light of God surrounds us;

The love of God enfolds us;

The power of God protects us;

The presence of God watches over us;

Wherever we are, God is!

How's that for a loving, caring, good Father who keeps watch over you and every intricate detail of your life? That poem is a great reminder that our God is surrounding us daily to be of strength to us, to protect us, and watch over us. God is everywhere we are. You're never alone. Wherever you are your journey, Daddy-God is there. It may not always feel like He's there but, as Freeman says: Wherever we are, God is!

Take time today to really and truly rest in your Daddy's hand today. How do you rest? By keeping your trust in Him, keeping your thoughts on Him, and totally relying on Him during the most fearful moments, situations, and circumstances. It may be finances, fertility, pregnancy, that next doctor's appointment, or upcoming test results that have you afraid and fearful. He reminds you to not be afraid because He'll be with you. Whatever the outcome, He's with you. He encourages you to not be discouraged, because He is your God; He's your Daddy and will strengthen, help, and hold you in His hands to cover and protect you when it becomes too much. He's not promising there won't be any hardships, but He is promising to keep you in His hands during the hardships.

Reflection & Application

1. What are you afraid of this time in your life?

2. What do you find most discouraging to you right now?

3. What does Isaiah 41:10 promise God will do for you?

Prayer Starter

God, you tell me in your word to not be afraid and discouraged because you are with me. You are my God. You even go on to say that you will strengthen me, help me, and hold me up with your victorious right hand. God, therefore, I will not be afraid or discouraged during my pregnancy or the ups and downs battling a diagnosis of infertility while trying to conceive my baby that I desire so much right now. I thank you for strengthening me during this time of feeling like I have no control over something that you created my body to do. I know that you are holding me up with your victorious right hand. Because of this, I can be confident in knowing that you are with me. I can also be confident in knowing that you are with me during all hardships and the not-so-good times, even when I feel alone. You're so faithful! In Jesus' name, amen!

Thoughts & Prayers

Thoughts & Prayers

Day 10

God Will Grant Your Request

*"'I asked the Lord to give me this boy, and he has granted my
request. Now I am giving him to the Lord, and he will belong to the
LORD his whole life.' And they worshiped the Lord there."*
1 Samuel 1: 27–28 (NLT)

The Bible contains numerous accounts of infertile women
having to deal with the struggle and pain of not being able
to have children. All of them trusted and believed God for their
babies—specifically boys—and God answered their prayers and
granted their request for a male child at the appointed time for
which they had a very important purpose from God to fulfill.

Hannah was one of these women. Hannah wanted a male child
so badly that she fasted and prayed. She desired motherhood
and began literally weeping and crying out to God—so much
so that the priest thought she was drunk. However, she made
her request known to God for motherhood through prayer and
fasting, and God granted her request.

The Bible tells us not to worry about anything and, instead, to pray about everything. Tell God what you need and thank Him for all He has done (Philippians 4: 6–7).

What can we learn from Hannah?

- She poured out her heart to God in prayer (1 Samuel 1:11, 15–16).

- She believed in the power of prayer and was confident in God's ability to answer her prayer (1 Samuel 1:17–18, 27).

Never stop praying and believing God for the impossible. And when we pray, we have to believe that he hears us, and will answer us. Matthew 19:26 (NLT), tells us "humanly speaking, it is impossible. But with God everything is possible".

Reflection & Application

1. What do you believe God for right now?

2. Do you find it difficult to believe He hears your prayers?

3. Read Hannah's story in 1 Samuel 1 and 2. Ask God to use this Bible story to reveal the power of prayer.

Prayer Starter

God, just as you answered Hannah's prayer for a son after many years of prayer, I believe that you will answer my prayer for a child. God, I give my unborn child back to you now, because he/she will be a testament of your glory and goodness. Thus, God I thank you in advance for hearing and answering my prayers. No matter how long I've been waiting, I will continue to pray and put my faith in you to answer. God, I come before you with a spirit of expectancy, waiting for you to answer my heart's desire. I stand on your word. I will be a mother just like Hannah! I thank you in advance! In Jesus' name, amen!

Thoughts & Prayers

Thoughts & Prayers

Renewed Faith

I know that walking this journey of motherhood is no easy thing to do. While many emotions consume your heart, mind, and spirit during infertility and pregnancy, it is my desire that these past 10 days you've been filled with hope, strength, faith, peace, confidence, and trust in our Father. I pray that the words from each day have grown you spiritually, and strengthened and renewed your faith like never before. Furthermore, my heart's desire is that you have gotten a clear understanding of what God has promised you through His word, and that you begin decreeing and declaring those promises for your life.

No longer just read the word, but speak it over your life and take ownership of it. Pray the word of God until you begin to believe what it says. Walk it out in your life, and allow it to drown the enemy's lies against your heart's desire for motherhood and a healthy pregnancy. Allow it to draw you closer to the God of miracles. Allow it to take root in your heart and transform the way you see God. You have to know His nature and know who He is before you can fully trust in Him, and His word.

After all, God's word is what changes things, and moves mountains that seem unmovable in our lives. I know, because as I began to pray and profess healing over my own life according to the word of God in 2015, that's when I began to see the manifestation of what I professed and believed God for. So, while I know this journey to motherhood during an infertility diagnosis is tough and painful, applying the word of God to fight fear during this time will lead you to a strengthened faith as you encounter a fearless journey to motherhood.

I've included two scripture-based prayers for you to fight fear during infertility and pregnancy. The *Prayer of Victory Over Infertility* was written in 2015 as Holy Spirit instructed me to not just memorize scriptures that would help me through my fertility journey while waiting on miracle baby number two, but to begin praying, decreeing, and declaring what God has spoken and promised me through His word. As a result, this prayer of victory and declaration was created. There's also the *Prayer for a Healthy, Full-Term Pregnancy.*

I'm sharing both with you on your journey to motherhood. Read these daily, and even consider writing your own and professing it aloud daily.

> "...I tell you the truth, if you had faith even as small as
> a mustard seed, you could say to this mountain, 'move

from here to there,' And it would move. Nothing would be impossible." (Matthew 17:20 NLT)

Prayer of Victory Over Infertility

My God, Father, and Creator,

I thank you for being the creator and giver of life. I thank you for being a God that opens and closes my womb. Lord, I thank you that I don't have to worry about my fertility and becoming a mother because I can pray instead, about all things, including motherhood. I thank you that when I pray about this situation I will experience your peace that will guard my heart and mind (**Philippians 4:6–7**). You will keep me in perfect peace as I trust you, and keep my thoughts and mind fixed on you (**Isaiah 26:3**). God, I thank you for leaving me the gift of peace of mind and heart. Your peace is a gift the world cannot give me. So, I will not be troubled or afraid (**John 14:27**). Lord, I also thank you for giving every childless, barren woman a family, making her a happy mother. So, thank you in advance for making me fruitful, fertile, healing my womb, and giving me a family (**Psalms 113:9**).

Your word says in **Hebrews 11:11** that it was by faith that even Sarah was able to have a child, though she was barren and was too old. She believed that God would keep His promise. So, God, I come putting my faith in you to conceive a child, although I've been diagnosed with infertility. I believe just like Sarah that you will keep your promise. And, just as the angel told Zechariah, "Don't be afraid!" I will not be afraid, Lord, because I know you have heard my prayer, just as you heard Zechariah's prayer for his wife, Elizabeth. I thank you in advance for the great joy and gladness, and how I will rejoice at my baby's birth (**Luke 1:13–14**)! Lord, therefore, I will not fear bad news; I will confidently trust you to care for me (**Psalms 112:7**). I thank you that your word says to don't be afraid, for you are with me. It says to not be discouraged, for you are my God. You will strengthen me and help me. You will hold me up with your victorious right hand (**Isaiah 41:10**). So, thank you for strengthening me when I'm tired. Thank you for helping me and holding me in your hands. You never let go of me. I will not walk in fear, worry, or doubt, but I will trust you, Lord. I will not be afraid!

Father God, Hannah stood praying to you and asked you to give her a baby boy. You granted her request and she gave him back to you, Lord, and her baby boy belonged to you his whole life (**1 Samuel 1:26–28**). I, too, am praying and asking you to give me my baby girl. I believe that you will, and I give her back to you, even now, before she's been conceived.

Lord, I serve you: the One and only God. I thank you for your provision over my life and protecting me from illness. Your word says that there will be no miscarriages or infertility, and you will give me a long, full life (**Exodus 23:25–26**). So, I speak life to come forth into my womb in Jesus' name. I take authority over the spirit of infertility, and command it to leave my body in Jesus' name! Daddy, I thank you that I am healed, I am fruitful, and I will conceive! In Jesus' mighty name! Amen!

Prayer for a Healthy, Full-Term Pregnancy

My God, Father, and Creator,

Thank you for this physical, tangible, manifestation of motherhood in my womb right now. Thank you for this precious miracle that you've blessed me with. You have created and formed this baby, and will cover and protect them in my womb (**Psalms 139:13 NLT**). I know that you are watching over this baby as he/she is growing and developing in my womb (**Psalms 139:15 NLT**). I was once childless, but you have made me a joyful mother (**Psalms 113:9 NLT**). Just like Hannah, I prayed and asked for this child, and you granted my request (**1 Samuel 1:27 NLT**). You blessed me with this gift of life inside of me. Thank you, God! Thank you for your faithfulness to me! As I rejoice in anticipation of birthing, holding, and nurturing this baby, I take authority over the spirit of fear trying to attack my mind and emotions at this happy time in my life. You keep me and my baby safe and sheltered from danger; you are a continuous and permanent help during trouble, and I will not fear (**Psalms 46:1–2 NLT**). Because you, God, remain with me and this child, keep us in your hands, and give me strength to carry this baby to full term, I have no reason to fear (**Isaiah 41:10 NLT**). You are my divine, supernatural, perfect peace, as I keep my focus on you, and who you are during the development, labor, and delivery of my child. You have created my and my baby's body to be strong and work together perfectly during labor and delivery (**2 Samuel 22:33 NLT**). Father, thank You for creating me in such a wonderful and complex way, so wonderful and complex that I can reproduce, conceive, carry, and birth my child. Thank you for creating me. Thank you for creating this baby inside of me. I submit this child back to you. Be glorified through my pregnancy and delivery! In Jesus' mighty name. Amen!

My Prayer Journal

Today I release fear of:

_____

_____

_____

_____

_____

_____

_____

_____

_____

_____

_____

_____

_____

_____

_____

_____

_____

_____

_____

_____

_____

_____

_____

_____

_____

_____

My Prayer Journal

*T*oday I release fear of:

_____

_____

_____

_____

_____

_____

_____

_____

_____

_____

_____

_____

_____

_____

_____

_____

_____

_____

_____

_____

_____

_____

My Prayer Journal

Today I release fear of:

_____

_____

_____

_____

_____

_____

_____

_____

_____

_____

_____

_____

_____

_____

_____

_____

_____

_____

_____

_____

_____

_____

_____

My Prayer Journal

*T*oday I release fear of:

_____

_____

_____

_____

_____

_____

_____

_____

_____

_____

_____

_____

_____

_____

_____

_____

_____

_____

_____

_____

_____

_____

_____

My Prayer Journal

Today I release fear of:

_____

_____

_____

_____

_____

_____

_____

_____

_____

_____

_____

_____

_____

_____

_____

_____

_____

_____

_____

_____

_____

_____

_____

_____

My Prayer Journal

*T*oday I release fear of:

_____

_____

_____

_____

_____

_____

_____

_____

_____

_____

_____

_____

_____

_____

_____

_____

_____

_____

_____

_____

_____

_____

_____

My Prayer Journal

*T*oday I release fear of:

_____

_____

_____

_____

_____

_____

_____

_____

_____

_____

_____

_____

_____

_____

_____

_____

_____

_____

_____

_____

_____

_____

_____

_____

_____

_____

_____

_____

My Prayer Journal

Today I release fear of:

_____

_____

_____

_____

_____

_____

_____

_____

_____

_____

_____

_____

_____

_____

_____

_____

_____

_____

_____

_____

_____

_____

_____

_____

_____

_____

My Prayer Journal

Today I release fear of:

_____

_____

_____

_____

_____

_____

_____

_____

_____

_____

_____

_____

_____

_____

_____

_____

_____

_____

_____

_____

_____

_____

_____

_____

My Prayer Journal

*T*oday I release fear of:

About the Author

Tiffany Finley is founder of My Predestined One, a faith-based nonprofit in Dallas, Texas, providing support, resources, education, and encouragement to women and couples affected by premature birth, and women and couples struggling to conceive due to an infertility diagnosis. She is also writer and blogger at TiffanyFinley.com, where she openly shares about her journey to motherhood after being diagnosed with polycystic ovarian syndrome in her mid-20s, later conceiving her rainbow baby (a former 25-week micro-preemie) via IVF/frozen embryo transfer after 14 months and two ectopic miscarriages, and offering hope and encouragement to her trying to conceive sisters and preemie moms. Currently, Tiffany is trying to expand her family of three to a family of four.

She enjoys family time, reading, shopping, binge watching Netflix, traveling, and leading worship. She lives in the Dallas–Fort Worth Metropolitan area, with her husband, Derek, to whom she's happily married, their son, Caleb, and their sweet dog, Duke.

Connect with Tiffany

Tiffany would love to connect with you, and support you on your fertility journey, while you walk and trust God on your fearless journey to motherhood. Visit her online at tiffanyfinley.com where you can subscribe to stay up to date with Tiffany's latest blog posts, special announcements, events, and faith-filled encouragement!

Facebook: Tiffany Finley

Instagram: Tiffany_Finley

Twitter: @TiffanyAFinley

Email: contact@tiffanyfinley.com (I would love to pray for you. Send your prayer requests.)

Connect with her ministry, My Predestined One, at mypredestinedone.org where you can subscribe to the newsletter to stay up to date with My Predestined One's events, in person & online infertility & preemie parent support groups, special announcements, latest blog posts, and encouraging stories of other women and couples who've been affected by infertility and premature birth, but God has given them strength and a testimony.

Facebook: My Predestined One

Online Facebook Support Groups:

My Predestined One: Fertility Support Group

My Predestined One: Preemie Parent Support Group

Instagram: My Predestined One

Twitter: @MyPredestined1

Email: contact@mypredestinedone.org (We would love to pray for you. Send your prayer requests.)